# Bisi Bee

## Sacrifice of a Remarkable Mother

Muyiwa Babalola Esq.

**Wasteland Press**
www.wastelandpress.net
Shelbyville, KY USA

*Bisi Bee:*
*Sacrifice of a Remarkable Mother*
by Muyiwa Babalola

Copyright © 2015 Muyiwa Babalola
ALL RIGHTS RESERVED

First Printing – March 2015
ISBN: 978-1-68111-017-2

NO PART OF THIS BOOK MAY BE REPRODUCED IN ANY FORM, BY PHOTOCOPYING OR BY ANY ELECTRONIC OR MECHANICAL MEANS, INCLUDING INFORMATION STORAGE OR RETRIEVAL SYSTEMS, WITHOUT PERMISSION IN WRITING FROM THE COPYRIGHT OWNER/AUTHOR

Printed in the U.S.A.

0   1   2   3   4   5   6   7   8

# DEDICATION

I dedicate 'Bisi Bee' to the memories of My Mum, Chief Mrs. Rachel Olabisi Babalola. She was a 'Busy Bee' all her life and her constant and undying love and support made the publication of this Book Possible.

I grew up reading My Mothers Poetry. The rhymes were simple yet inviting. She wrote like she sat next to you. She made Poetry Fun and I caught on to it early. For Several years, she published her poetry in the Nigerian Baptist Magazines at a time when most women were seen and not heard, she wrote loudly and clearly with her Pen to a large audience.

She also authored several books on Nursing, Midwifery, Marriage, Devotionals and an Autobiography titled 'Christiana's only Child'.

She taught me the art of giving without expecting anything back in return. I accompanied her on several trips where she fed the Homeless and ministered to their needs in ways that remain fresh in my mind.

My Mum hailed from a humble background. She was sent to live with relatives at Minna Nigeria. Fluent in Hausa and hawking goods to earn her stay and board. She maintained her innocence, dignity and academic excellence through the dint of hard work.

Mama R.O.B, as she was fondly called, was an accomplished academician and Lifetime member of the West African College of Nursing. She was Principal of School of Midwifery UCH, for over two Decades, mentoring thousands of nurses and midwives excelling around the World. I still meet several Nursing practitioners that express their love and admiration for the Mentoring influence of my Mum.

How do I say Thank you to an amazing mother? By living every day worthy of the tremendous sacrifice she made. I saw her on bended knees several times interceding for her children, praising through very tough situations and never letting go.

You dwelt in discomfort for our ultimate comfort. There are times when I wonder how you made all the right calls, most of the time. The answer lies in the room of prayer. I am comforted by the fact that you are rejoicing with the host of Heaven. Keep praising at the Pearly gates.

I am extremely blessed to have called you 'Mum'. If every mother was like you, the world will be a better place to live. I Miss and Love you so Much.

M.B.

# ACKNOWLEDGEMENTS

I acknowledge the presence and Help of the Almighty God for his grace, wisdom, and protection over my Life. For the countless numbers of times, that I called and He answered. I am indeed grateful.

I am grateful for the sacrificial, unending, exemplary love from my Parents, Chief Isaac Dokun Babalola Esq. and Chief Mrs. Rachel Olabisi Babalola, who shared the true essence of Life and was unashamed of their Faith. You are the best Parents in the World and I will not exchange you for any other. You nurtured beautiful children through the dint of hard work and determination. Mummy, I will miss you so much. Your words, prayers flow through my veins. Your memories are fresh and everlasting. I know that you are in Heaven singing your favorite Hymns. You are a Diamond of Inestimable value.

To my Lovely wife, Dolapo Apinke Babalola for the Support and guidance from the first day I laid eyes on you at the Video rental store in Bodija Ibadan, you have been a pillar of support.

How can I forget my awesome children? Mayowa, Moyosola and Daraju who's little hearts encompass all the Love needed to make the world go round. You are the reason I continue to strive for greatness on a daily basis. Your smile makes me melt into your lovely arms.

To my Mother in Law, Mrs. Funmilayo Adeoshun, you are like a tree planted by the side of the river that keeps giving. We appreciate and love you very much. To the Adeoshuns at large, Bunmi and Folorunsho Akingbade, Bukola and Omo Adeoshun, Seyi Adeoshun, Adekeye's and Obidike's. Thank you for the Support through the years.

My story will not be complete without the contributions made by my high school Literature teacher, Mr. Sanyaolu (Skiddo). He constantly saw in me a gem that was not immediately visible and carefully guided me to the right path.

My Brothers and Sisters; Dr Mrs. Yetunde Ayo-Bello, Prof Femi Babalola, Christopher Babalola, Elizabeth Ukor, Abiodun Babalola and Paul

Babalola. The Bands and affection over the years can never be compensated. I owe an immense debt of gratitude for your protection, warmth, support and presence in my life.

The Lero Clan, resident and in the Diaspora, Sanya Otuyalo (Stiga), Femi Afolabi (Afoo), Yinka Kushemiju (Kush), Taiwo Bada (T-Bad), Tayo and Tolu Ogun, Mide Ademidun (Atila), Folabi Akinpelu (Pucla), Emmanuel Olali, Bunmi Alalade (Gannucci), Wole Ajibade (Jibad), Yinka Olajuwon, Olumide Kayode, Timi Balogun and You.

To my Uncles and Aunts; Prof Sanjo & Josephine Bode, Prof Bayo & Grace Oyekan, Dr Soji Giwa, Dr Lexy Oyeyinka, Dr Ndi Okwuosa, Layo Omotosho, Prof Tunji Omotara, Remi Omotara, Bolaji Omotara, Titi Omotara, Dr Biyi & Ronke Odugbesan. I appreciate the positive influence you have had on my life. I am truly grateful.

To my In Laws; Dr. Ayo-Bello, Idowu Babalola, Ebong Ukor, Christy Babalola and Joke Babalola. You have all shared the innermost reaches of your love. As you were there for me, I will be there for you.

My Pastors; David Cooper and Korede Akindele. The Spiritual Nuggets planted in my life are yielding dividends in multiple dimensions.

To the entire AAA Parking Family, International Systems Strategies and Olajide Oyewole & Co Law Firm and Wale Babalakin & Co Law Firm. I am indebted for developing my Legal and professional acumen.

To my Friends too numerous to mention, Professional Colleagues and acquaintances, may our connections grow stronger.

M.B

# TABLE OF CONTENTS

A Mother in the Calm of the Night ................................................. 1
A Reflection on Black History .......................................................... 3
A Way to Please ................................................................................. 5
All in a Box ......................................................................................... 6
An Offering of Thanksgiving ............................................................. 8
Bisi Bee ............................................................................................. 11
Commander in Peace ...................................................................... 13
Conflict Listening ............................................................................ 16
Daraju ............................................................................................... 18
Dear Dad .......................................................................................... 20
Director ............................................................................................ 22
Dolly Pop .......................................................................................... 23
Extra Dose of Insulin ...................................................................... 24
Flight Dana ...................................................................................... 26
From Geology to Theology ............................................................. 28
Germs! .............................................................................................. 31
Healthy Dose of Americana ........................................................... 34
Hurricane Irene ............................................................................... 37
I Don't Want To ............................................................................... 39
I Tried to Let It Go .......................................................................... 41
In Search of Peace .......................................................................... 42
Is It Over? ........................................................................................ 43
Iya Abiye of Igbajo-Land ................................................................. 44
Jokilicious ........................................................................................ 46
Just Bloom ....................................................................................... 48
Life in Seconds ................................................................................ 50
Little Steps ....................................................................................... 51
Love Speaks Louder than Words ................................................... 53
Luger Nodar Kumaritashvili ........................................................... 56
Our Love is Here to Stay ................................................................. 58
Macabre Dance ................................................................................ 59
Mother Nile ...................................................................................... 61
Mountains ........................................................................................ 63
Moyosola .......................................................................................... 64
My Favorite Blanket ........................................................................ 65
Mayowa ............................................................................................ 67

| | |
|---|---|
| Oil Spill in the Gulf | 70 |
| The Queen of Oprah | 72 |
| Rachel | 74 |
| Remove the Training Wheels | 76 |
| Secret Chambers of the Heart | 78 |
| Segun Sege | 80 |
| Split Personality | 82 |
| Summer Breeze | 84 |
| Superwoman's Creed | 86 |
| Texting and Driving | 88 |
| The Ayo-Bello Legacy | 89 |
| The Best of Times, the Worst of Times | 92 |
| The Green Grass | 93 |
| The Hark and the Heralds | 95 |
| A Heart of Stone | 97 |
| The Kiln of Purification | 99 |
| The Leaks of Wiki | 101 |
| The Love That Once Was | 103 |
| The Making of a Mother | 105 |
| The Man Stored Within | 107 |
| The March into Greatness | 109 |
| The Orchids of Catalina | 111 |
| The Presence of Absence (9-11) | 113 |
| The Telephone | 115 |
| To Tie The Knot? | 116 |
| Valet Driver | 118 |
| What a Year! | 120 |
| Where Do I Start? | 123 |
| Who is This Boy? | 124 |

# A Mother in the Calm of the Night

In the calm of the night
There was always one with sight
Thoroughly thoughtful, never in doubt
The heartaches, headaches and shouts,
Never drowned the one still voice.

She gave her best,
But her best was not good enough.
He saw himself in a tiny frame.
She imagined him in an entire gallery.
The contract was for better or worse?
All she got was the worst and the end of the barrel.

Most people encouraged her to leave.
Abandon him and start all over.
Give him a taste of his own medicine.
Let him experience life without your help and attention.

Forget his love and pursue love on the other side.
I stopped for a second, Looked at my children and concluded,
Life will always be better for them with a man they call Dad.
Why are women left to make the tough choices?

Forced to support the Family
Life just seems to be so unfair.
Grinding to the never-ending
Demands of a world
That does not listen.

Emptying themselves to men they barely knew.
Wondering how they made such poor choices.
Women bare scars in their hearts.
The passage of time dulls the pain.
A once beautiful rose is now pressed down.

Abandoned dreams
And broken promises.
I thought that I would fly through the ends of the earth with you?
I ended up barely able to walk around the block without a cane.

Several babies, after all said and done
And all she got from him was exactly none
She picked so much bone
The plan was for the best of time
All she got was the worst of time.

She really did try,
Through the years she cried
He scoffed, buffed and left her tired
The way of life seemed so unfair.

She dusted herself and laced her boots
Like the phoenix she rose
One brick at a time
A good foundation for the kids she laid.

The destination was quite far
But in time she caught the stars
Glittering through the night
Alas a beautiful morning to share.

## A Reflection on Black History

It's that time of the Year
We salute the greatness of our Lineage
We celebrate the Heritage that lies within us,
Looking back at the strength of our Ancestry.
Casting our nets to catch the wisdom of our forbearers.

They fought a good fight.
A path was laid for you and me.
Starting with nothing but a dream,
They imagined a world full of love, hope and acceptance.

They charted a course through barren Lands.
They were fortified by the passion for a better tomorrow.
They marched, invented and expounded the viewpoint of the past
They crafted and sculpted a new dawn for a new day.

Harriet Tubman, Langston Hughes, W.E.B Dubois, Andrew Young,
John Lewis, Oprah Winfrey, Barrack Obama and Martin Luther King Jr.
Just to mention a Few, were pioneers who trailed a path.
We are more than our skin color,
We are members of the Human race.

We look to the past as a guide for the direction of the Future.
We hope for a light at the end of the tunnel.
We forge ahead against the odds and the obstacles,
Assured that we can always borrow,
From the wisdom
Of the future.

We appreciate the sacrifice and the selflessness.
Instead of stopping, they persevered.
Despite the injustice, they stood tall
And kept moving toward the promise land.

I pledge to live to the essence of their sacrifice
To make their mission my mission,
Spreading the truth in love,
To create a better place
For all humanity.

It's not just Black History,
It is our history.
Happy black history month!

## A Way to Please

She knew the way to Please.
Her way was nice and sweet.
The way was straight not bent.
There is a way, in her sway,
She gave way to a humble heart.
She bent, swept but still went her way.
Her smile shined brighter than the Milky Way.

A believer, a true believer,
First Vic member she was,
Great Mum, a super Mum,
She kept like the mother Hen.

The way of the Cross-she knew.
She knew the way. Do you?
My true and Faithful servant,
to the bosom of the Lord to rest.

Eating with Abraham,
Dinning with Jesus,
What a wonderful way to spend Eternity.
Gone far away, to a land of Joy, peace, singing and Laughter.

Weep not.
My Lady's in a good place.
The Early flight she took.
I tell you...........
Without a doubt..........
The way of the cross
was her Way.

# All in a Box

All I ever did, all I ever accomplished
All my awards, gifts and honors
All my love and lust
All the wealth, knowledge
All the work,
Lots of work.

The houses, cars, boats and land
The sandy beaches, the rolling waves
The memories, thoughts and doubts
The women, children and concubines
All gave way for a box.

I was guided on the right path
The means to an end became the end to a means
I delayed the flow of the windy streams.

I tasted the marrows of several dry bones
The victories lost on the ivy top
Scuttled by the all
Encompassing size of my box.

Smartness was my key to wealth
Everlasting riches in Gold and myrrh
Immaculate rows of chapters unfold.
Never costing me more than my easy pen
I thought I owned the golden egg and the hen
Until I found myself
Six feet under in a box.

The box was laden with fine wood
The handles adorned with the choice of silver
The locks were latches made from China
Insignias on the side came from the coast of Ghana
Was it really fit for a box?

The toast of town were my bosom friends
The chamberlains and the shakers were on my lane
As I grew older, I learnt to walk on a cane
I tried to give as much of my fame away
Before the knock came to lie in the box.

I look around and wonder
At all the fountains I never saw
The roses and splendor of nature
Seas and Oceans bashing against the riverbank
Wondering why I never had it in my memory bank.

It's quiet in the tiny box
Much smaller than my pet house
Not fitting for the local Indian Chief
My feathers hanging on a wall
Far away from
My longest reach.

How do you get out of the box?
Do I stay locked forever?
My skin has started faltering
The worms are excited at the thoughts of dinner
Nobody makes it out alive!

# An Offering of Thanksgiving

What a day, what a wonder?
Another opportunity to be all I can be
I switch the gears and count the cost
Somebody paid at the cross just for me
To roam and
Hold my peace.

I was once young and each day I grow
In the knowledge of the one that made it all
We speak and declare the emptiness of our thoughts
Waiting patiently at the behest of his Omniscience.

Once is never enough
Humanity tries to acquire all the gold
Until we discover the futility of the golden calf
We stretch our imagination and build countless dreams
Instead of looking unto the creator
 Who rules and reigns Supreme.

At the beginning of the year
I made resolutions I promised to keep
Breaking every single one as I went along
Staring at the futility, I rest in the one who is able.

Many times I drive along the busy highways
Stringing through wide expanse of Tar
I change lanes and increase my speed
Weaving through traffic and coming to a standstill
Hoping to arrive at the destination faster
I stop today, and realize, it was only by his Omnipotence.

Our families are precious in his eyes
He made us a part and not apart
He imparted in us his word to abide
Seeking always to reside in his love.

The latitude of our transgressions are far and wide
Where do we begin to take stock of our erring ways?
The lies we told and the hate we hold
Of all the creatures Almighty Jehovah made
He looks and laughs and forgives us all the same.

The blessings He gave cannot be counted
The rain and the seeds are one of such reasons
We eat and drink and yet so many do without
The basics we have and take for granted
No matter your state or station give an offering of thanks.

A reason to give thanks to the one who sees it all
For the joy of laughter
The gift of sadness
The aptitude for attitude
The reason for the season
The miles we walked.

The opportunity for repentance
The accidents barely missed
The happiness of a newborn
The celebrations of milestones
The promotions and not demotions
The demotions and not cremations.

The loss of a father and adoption of the heavenly father
The imaginations through a sound mind
The ability to breathe in the freshness of God
The hands to hold and to behold
The clock that ticks and order seems to exist.

The world that is in flux and not reflux
The thoughts of goodness and loving-kindness
The fervent and effective prayers of brethren.

The acknowledgement of the Omnipresence of his Eminence
The hope for a better
And brighter tomorrow.
I bow at his feet with an offering thanksgiving.

## Bisi Bee

A mother is a pearl of immeasurable Value
That you cannot buy with wads of Money.
She carried me in her womb for Nine Months,
She carried me on her back for 3 years
A mother is a pearl of Immeasurable Value
That wads of Money cannot Buy.

Rachel Olabisi Babalola
Was a diamond of Immeasurable value.
A powerhouse
In a little frame.

She nurtured her kids with love and affection.
She reminded us that
'Service to Humanity is the best work of life'.
An only child and a survivor in every way;
Olabisi left a void that only God can fill.

My mother was a 'Bisi Bee' all her life
Climbing to the very pinnacle of the Nursing Profession,
Mentoring thousands
And serving the sickly
Around the world.

She thought us that with God on our side,
Who can be against us?
Always working, always busy.
She reminds me of the Bumble Bee.

True mothers are in short supply.
A mother is selfless and loving
Sharing her love in equal increments
Yet, expecting no reward.

They are mothers to the Father,
Children, relations and workers.
A full day's sleep is always in short supply.
Toiling away on the never-ending tasks.

Bisi Bee was always on bended knees.
Praying for one and all.
Adopting children all of persuasions.
Number Five Afolabi Durotoye Street,
Always had a plate and a place for all our Friends.

My mother passed on to glory at a healthy age.
Her memories will remain fresh in my mind forever.
She touched me in ways that are indescribable.

Her words rings true everywhere I go.
She is not gone because a part of her is always in us.
Anytime you see a Bumble Bee,
Look carefully; it might just be 'Bisi Bee'.

# Commander in Peace

My name is Barrack Hussein Obama.
I am the 'Commander in Peace' of the Armed Forces.
The greatest legacy a man can leave,
Is Peace within and peace without?

Most will say Blow them, Bomb them,
Lock them up and throw the keys away.
I will say instead that true
Communication yields lasting peace.

The Nobel peace prize came to me.
I did not ask for it.
War should be the last option and not the first.
No one truly wins; we are all casualties of War.
It's easy to go to war and difficult to get out.

Several are maimed for life.
For causes sometimes they least understand.
Promising careers cut short by hurried decisions,
Made by those who will barely fire a single bullet.

Most made the sacrifices knowing the possibilities.
Fighting for Freedom and a way of life.
A right to life, love and
Live in a land that embraces all.

Sharing sacred and inalienable values
That flows through our veins.
The grass of Freedom was watered
By the blood and sacrifices of our Forbearers.

From Gaithersburg, Normandy,
Vietnam and the gates of Baghdad.
Freedom is costly
The currency is shed on the battlefields.

I am not naïve to think that there is no Evil in the world.
All you have to do is look around you
And you'll find them in abundance.
Staring you in the face and plotting untold evil.
The question is always, what do you do in return?

A school of thought will say they are different from us.
They celebrate evil and abhor democratic values.
They profess a religion that is rooted
And grounded in violence.

It's always a question of
Let him that is without Sin, cast the first stone?
There were times when all faiths made regrettable decisions,
Made a wrong turn or refused to turn the other cheek.

Humanity has always been a race for dominance.
No one stays on top forever.
The first is the last and the last is the first.
We must constantly re-invent
Ourselves to remain relevant.

We hold these truths to be self-evident.
That all Men are created equal
One nation, Indivisible under God
 With Unity and Justice for all.

I am Black and white at the same time.
I am African and Caucasian.
I am a melting pot of races and culture.
I love more when I am reviled.
Love always conquers hate.

From Selma to Ferguson,
Peaceful Demonstrations
With varying outcomes.

Nothing is promised on a platter of Gold.
Challenges abound at every corner
Despite our frailties, we still remain the United States of America.

We are the custodians of those that have past.
We owe a debt that we choose to pay forward.
There is nothing more pressing than the urgency of now.
Resolving unfolding crises with a blessed Assurance
That blessed are the Peacemakers,
For they will be called the Children of God.

## Conflict Listening

We need to listen.
It's a skill that is sorely lacking
A lack of it breaks our home and ruins corporations
And separates a church from the parishioners.
Away to your tent and cast your lot
I wish we could zip it and sip it just for a second.

A lack of it is a bane of government
Elected leaders vow to listen
To Capital hill they flock
They become tone- deaf around the block.

The clock ticks, the kick come and goes
We hope for the click
But it's really nothing but a flick.
We are born to listen.

To be calm and absorb all the sense
And make sense of all the noise
It's not a game of cat and mouse
All because
We do not listen.

Samuel did it in the middle of the night
We can start when it's nice and bright
When we do, we can fly as a kite
The bite is gone, the sight is clear.

It helps to build bridges
It mends broken relationships and lives
It alleviates the need for armed conflict
Listening crafts a new era of a rainbow fortification
Of divergent views and opinions.
Making us stronger as a Unit.
We climb walls and pull down strongholds

We tear the veil of confusion that envelopes
Creating fear and torment that cripples
It becomes a never-ending torrent of monosyllables
Never sums up to a dialogue.

I stand on the mountaintop of conscience
I run to the streams of eloquence
I borrow from the buckets of wisdom
I sip into the bowels of history
The unending cracks of opportunity.

Listening is a sweet wall
The tall and adaptable grass
It waves and moves and bends as the wind blows
It bows, but never breaks at the gust of the Hurricane.

The complete rhapsody of reason
The unending chasm of essence
It escapes the truism of reality
It's blind to the call made on Main Street
All it seems to suggest is 'this is my street'
A one-way street.

To truly listen, you stop
Your eyes are fixed and steady
You assimilate and analyze
Not breaking in or interrupting.

The streams slowly following its path
To the fields of fresh flowers ever blossoming
At the supply of the fresh waters
Of the valley of the monks.
Listen.
Learn to listen.

# Daraju

Today is not a celebration of Life.
It is a celebration of the faithfulness of the Almighty.
Once He says it will be, there is a path set toward his will.
He is the author, finisher,
And rewarder of those that diligently seek Him.

We hold in our arms a bundle of joy.
Oluwadaraju is his name meaning
'The Lord is the very best'.
If you doubt it, I invite you to taste Him
And you will see that it is true.
He is the One who specializes in impossibilities.

Daraju was born on our wedding anniversary.
I was away at work when I got the call.
'Your wife is in the Hospital' Mummy Adeoshun said.
I dropped all my plans, raced from downtown
To the suburbs of Marietta.

It seemed like it took forever
To get to kennestone Hospital,
By the time I arrived,
Dolapo was adorned with lots of Drips.

I knelt down,
Prayed to the almighty for keeping an eye always.
She said, 'Go home, and put the Girls in bed'.
It will be a long night.

I picked some Chic-Fila on the way home
And read them a good night story.
My heart was beating to irregular rhythms of joy and haste.
By the time I arrived the Contractions had progressed.
My wife's breathing had a clear sense
Of urgency as I slowly pressed her arms.

Before the clock struck twelve,
All heavens broke loose.
Doctors and Nurses,
Little and big surrounding her Bed.
I saw it all and it seemed so surreal.
His head forced its way out and I knew the time was nigh.

With a little push, he came out as bright as can be.
He cried a little as they wrapped him in white blue and green.
His eyes opened for a minute as if to say
'Hey what's going on?'
I shed a tear when I meditated on the goodness of the Almighty.

Weighing seven and one ounces with lots of hair,
I welcomed Daraju with admiration and amazement.
We named him Shalom meaning peace.
He will be a peacemaker wherever he goes.
The mark of the excellence of the Lord will be with him.

Daraju, Shalom Babalola
 Is a blessing to our household.
He eats on demand and poops ever so often.
As we celebrate today.

We should all remember the giver of life now and always.
He is the architect of our lives and the anchor of our hopes.
Welcome Daraju to the land of endless possibilities.
We truly love you and always will.

## Dear Dad

I looked up and grabbed your hands.
My small fingers
Nestled in your huge hands.
You thought me to dig
Not to stop but always grab the fig
That opens up and leads to the big and bigger.

I looked up to you for guidance
You led me to the May dance
I fell often and your strong hand held me up
My first fall on my bike was before your eyes.

To walk like you, talk like you and live like you
Will be the challenge on the way to being you
I miss the afternoon walks, the day gone fishing
The ride to the football game
 And several trips to your office.

You thought me to pray and not prey
On the defenseless and the weak
You lead me to be confident and move
Toward the goal just beyond the cove
Always the peaceful dove.

Stay away from the curse words
Keep your words and mind your words
They have legs and take you near or far
It makes some and breaks most.

The money was good
The cars were neat
The houses were impressive
The trips were fun.

The schools were unique
The love from you was
What I remember the most
It's what I cherished and still hold dear.

Thank you for the vision for the stars
Not merely settling for the sky
To strive to be the best in all I think and do
And having a listening spirit to love
The best is what you are and always will be
My dad.

# Director

To activate, you need to act
To be heard, you need to speak
To learn, you need to read.

To know, you need to meditate
To reach, you need to stretch
To sleep, you need to shut your eyes.

To rise, you need to arise
To fly, you need winds under your wings
To walk, you need to take steps.

To achieve, you need to strive
To have a great movie, you need to direct it all.

# Dolly Pop

It was a bright sunny day
In a place where movies are leased
Our fates had a date
That will last and last and last.

You smiled and the lights were brighter
You laughed and the mood was lighter
The white pants were nice and snuggly
Just like a teddy bear you were lovely.

I said hello, and you smiled
Your hello was soft and gentle
All I wanted was to know the princess
Who was the source of my fairy tale?

Once upon a time
In a far away land
Was all I could hear?
I have been awe struck by the princess
Whose lollipop was bound to impress
Who is this Dolly pop?
That will always be my lollipop.

# Extra Dose of Insulin

My friend is a diabetic
Out of a job and on state rolls
never fitting in everywhere she goes
accepting her faith as nemesis from above.

The medications are always present
Trips to the Pharmacy were fairly frequent
Trying hard to be a great Parent
Realizing that her best intentions had limitations.

There are days she tries to run
only to fall facing the Sun
Her strength is faint and that is not fun
and her skin slowly changes its tone.

Molly was on her way out and she felt numb
She forgot her shots and it was dumb
the feeling was crippling comparable to bread crumbs
Pieces of her Body simply refused commands.

I will fight this foe
Education has proven to be a vital tool
Adhering to the best meals and plans
I jump, hide and run through hoops in my backyard.

The shot of insulin gave me an instant high
The energy level was instant and out of sight
Alert and able to be the very best can be
A miracle juice that makes me feel all right.

The weight has always been a problem
My heart pumps at rates faster than it should
My knees are fussing from the daily grind
I moan loudly as I slowly move around.

I am wiser now
The carbs have given way to veggies and fruits
Less sugar and more salads and healthy juices
Suddenly, the fat are dropping before my eyes.

The best revenge for Diabetes is change
My thoughts and the way I view myself
Making healthy choices in exchange for
Years of a happy and healthy life.

A new dawn is here
A bright day shining brighter as it evolves
showing promising changes as it revolves
The Sun and Moon in equal rotations
I realize that I don't have to depend on a daily dose of Insulin
To the new me, I say 'cheers'.

## Flight Dana

It was a flight to nowhere
In a country that is not going anywhere
Ruled by People who think anyhow
For determined populace everywhere.

I weep for my Country anyhow
Hoping that Somebody,
Somewhere, anywhere will say.
Enough of the bitterness, sorrow and oppression.

In a Land blessed with plenty but lacking much.
Souls perishing for no justifiable reason
Cocoa, Oil, Timber, Rubber, Bauxite flourish
Within a Country blessed with two Seasons.

I weep for thee, my Country.
I wish you growth but you remain stunted.
Avarice and Nepotism rules in the Jungle of Wazobia
We have become a comedy in the Diaspora.

When will we get there, I beg to ask?
In a thousand, million or billion years?
What do we need to do to wake you up from your slumber?
We seem to slide down a slippery slope.
We have Hope and we pray much.

One-Day Justice will arise and the people shall be free
From the Daily struggles and manic tussles.
We implore the earth to yield its own
the day oil flowed was the day soil ceased.

Take back the oil
Give me a country filled with compassion and hope.
Nigeria will rise again, like the sphinx we will rise
From the ashes of yesteryears

The souls of the departed will arise and
Call forth the fountains of Justice.
No Matter how much money, Goods and Possessions are stolen;
We will always yield more and not less.
The confluence of the River Niger shall not be broken
you will one day see us attain true greatness.

The true wealth of a nation is not the sum of its Goods
But the inner strength and peace of the populace
And, I assure you that it can never be stolen
No matter how they try.

The memories of the departed lives on,
Ask not for whom the bell tolls, for it tolls for thee.
Flight Dana, we will always remember thee.
We cry not, because we faint not
Our path shines brighter and brighter until the perfect light.

# From Geology to Theology

Mesh is such a smash.
A friend in time
And a friend in need.
Coming from Humble roots
Climbing all the way through various tours
He found his passion at the doorway of Praise.

I met him at Ife, Great Ife.
Always hailing me as 'Bablo'.
I first heard about him while at Rockshock Magazine
Looking at him was not a culture shock.

He was always at the white house
Not the one in Washington, but the science Building
At the Obafemi Awolowo University
Studying and complaining at the same time
Saying 'Ise Yi ti le Juu'.

Kunle is a Pastor Now
But at that time he was with the boys
We all were. Coming From Middle class Backgrounds
Privileged but leveraged with Grounded training.

Kunle knew his limits and never crossed it.
While walking the Halls of Oduduwa Hall
He will bring different beats
He has always been gifted in Music.

Then we graduated and left to serve
Serving a country we least understood
Getting confused at the utter recklessness of our leaders.
We called it quits and left the shores of the Country.

I met him at Redeemed at the Atl.
I was walking around minding my Business
And I heard 'The Bablo'
There was only one person in the World who called me that.
La Mesh!

He met a lovely Damsel.
Smitten at First Sight by her Voluptuous Looks
Ravaged by her Sultry Voice
Captivated by her Smile.
It was the 90's and they fell in Love.

Vivian, Eloho Meshida
Was meant for my guy.
No matter how little they had, she loved him just the same.
Summer, Rain or winter, She remained the same.
I was the Best Man and it was special.
It was a love made to last.

He found his passion.
Music was his passion.
He rationalized and had a choice to make,
Geology or theology.
He chose Musicology with Theology.

Just like David, He chose to Praise.
He realized that praise breaks down Boundaries
No Weapon formed against you shall prosper.

With Praise the walls of Jericho came down.
With Praise the Children of Israel crossed the Red Sea.
With Praise the Enemy flees in Several Directions.
With Praise we invite the presence of the Almighty.

He dumped geology and Climbed to theology.
He can praise you and make you part with Dollars
He can praise and usher
 His presence into your surroundings.

La Mesh, You remain a loyal and true Friend.
I Love and Honor
Your entire Family today
As we celebrate your Climb to Forty.
Now that you are there
Keep Climbing
The Best is yet to come.

## Germs!

Five letters that carry so much punch
They gather in bunches around the branches
All shapes, colors and sizes
They lurch and lie in wait for the unassuming fella
Masquerading and camouflaging
 Around the water fountain.

We can't see them, but they roll like dice.
Roll them and it may fall on all sides.
Microscopic in scope and flowing like a tide
They come ashore often with different waves
Beneath the seas, the lock ness hides.

Is it in the soil, air water or cup?
Its everywhere you touch
And all over the couch
The commode and the bathtub
The pouch you have and hold
Nice it may be, they spy for the germs.

They adapt easily to new environments
Sometimes they play hide and seek
Mostly wrecking havoc to the host they invade
They reside under the canopy of the weak and restless.

Awaiting the call to arms
They overtake all the defenses
They crush and blast until they recoil
Accepting the germs as the new Thomas Kincaid.

They love the air and stay airborne
Some swim in the water and take on the name Hydro
A few only spread with a hug or a touch
Mischievous ones perch on foods and drinks and lay some eggs.

We have done a lot to understand these strange fellows
Through a scholarly program called Epidemiology
We discover, contain and prevent the occurrence
Reducing the risks and discovering the source
Vaccines and tablets keep the germs at bay.

Eradication is a word that comes with a price
Fighting the forces that change and mutate
Sustaining the very best fight it can muster
It breaks away and spread the tentacles of fame
Germs simply stated with our best effort are here to stay.

Several countries have known the scourge
From the Bubonic plague across the sea
To Cholera and measles in many regions
Diphtheria once landed on the Asian Pacific.

Germs adapt and move with the wind
 Thanks to the Center for Disease Control
They contain and reduce the factor of germs
Isolating and understanding our brethren in vials
Anti-bodies help fight the scourge and limit the spread.

Some say to prevent is the key to success
Drinking clean water and boiling our food
Covering the meat at the market place
Sweeping away the stagnant water in the yard.

Can they be stopped?
Should they be destroyed?
What good are they anyway?
What is the fuss all about?
I'll tell if you listen.
They cost so much once it spreads
Once smitten, productivity lessens
Children call off and smile less
Others cry and groan in pain
The clinic livens up with needles and syrups.

Penicillin and anti-biotic
Saline mixes and water bottles
Cough syrups and chest ointments
Ear drops and eye drops
Band-aids
Across the chin.

For all the bad, germs also do some good
Some bacteria are cultivated developed into anti-bodies
A few reside in our intestines and helps with digestion
They ripen the Cheese and make it a delicacy
I guess there are several sides to the coin.

The world of germs is not for the faint hearted
A complex place with complex terms
No matter the effort we provide
The ball seems to roll further downstream.
We sweat and toil with the weight and strain
Germs can never go down the drain.

# Healthy Dose of Americana

I was born within the shores of the United States
My Parents hail from the shores of the North East
I recite the National Anthem and pledge every day
Every step I take, I remember the sacrifices made
Long before we were called the United States
I am more American than you.

I fly the flag on the front porch of my home
My favorite tie has the colors of white, blue and red
My bumper sticker urges us all to support our troops
I walk all day in my one and only boots
I am more American than you.

I am a Christian and don't you forget
I treat my neighbor as my self
To church I go every other Sunday
The Lord's Prayer is my constant companion
I keep the Sabbath and keep it Holy
I am more American than you.

I will never leave the shores of this country
No other can ever represent what we hold dear
We are the greatest in all we do
The richest and the brightest
All others send their best to our land
I am more American than you.

I eat grits in the morning
Barbecue in the afternoon
Corn on the cob in the evening
The south is where we call home
We fought the civil war
And bear the scars to show
I am more American than you.

I love the I pod and live on Face book
I tweet and feel at home with Hip-Hop.
My pants constantly hang below my waistline
The latest sneakers are mine to hold and have
My ride is decked with speakers and a sub-woofer
I am more American than you.

I work hard and care for the aged
I am a chip from the old block
I am prim and proper
Always sitting on the table for supper
I am more American than you.

My name is easy to pronounce
It's definitely easy on the ears
I look right and talk right
There are no accents in my speech
I am more American than you.

I have enlisted in the Military
My Father was ex-Military
I love the Army and will make any needed sacrifice
I ship out anytime I am called to active duty
My goal is three tours of duty
To silence the enemies of our Homeland
I am more American than you.

I own a home
I carry a mortgage against my name
I own two vehicles and two kids
I mow my lawn and owe credit loans
I am more American than you.

I swear and use curse words
I swing and sway as I move along
It's so easy for me to get along
I eat burgers and hot-dog and sing a song
The fries I eat are cut in squares.
I am more American than you.

I own a Business and pay my workers
I pay my taxes and spend during the Seasons
I vote during every election come sun or rain
It gives me the opportunity to show my disdain
I am more American than you.

What really makes you an American?
Is it by birth or ethnic origin?
Could it be the status of your wealth?
Or the section
Of your Estate?
Your looks name or color?
The flag you fly and what you wear when you go by?

What really makes you more American than me?
To be American is truly a privilege and not a right.
What you make out of it depends on whom you ask
Is it a concept or a way of life?

A declaration made on a summer afternoon?
Words read while witnesses' watch and cheer?
Take a pill of a healthy dose of America
What makes you an American depends on you.

## Hurricane Irene

It was a clear summer day when Irene made Landfall.
Heralded as a Hurricane three but came in as one.
The wind Gust was over a Hundred miles an hour
All the things that lay on its part were made cowards.

The majesty of the sway was like no other
The smallest toddler will not easily forget it.
There were several sirens in the wake of Irene.
Houses were leveled and bridges were flattened.

The rivers and streams swelled until it bust in its seams.
The vegetation and the farmland lost the beam of freshness
Strange items were dropped at my footsteps from hundreds of miles.
I ask everyone around when the strange tide will level and stop.

In the midst of it, lives were saved
Children found their parents once again
The rain we once dreamed and prayed for was here.
The earth that was hungry for water has been fed to overflowing
New plants will grow and barren lands are now fertile again.
Despite the loss of lives and goods,
We still have reason to smile.

All is not lost at the behest of Irene.
We choose to move on despite the hand dealt
There will always be a rainbow after the Landfall of Irene
Just like Irene, the season is changing once again.

The leaves that were once vibrant will fall and die.
Fertilizing the vegetation for the season that lay ahead.
Despite the loss of greenery, we see the beauty of the twigs
The leaves change and display the full array of colors.

Beautiful shades of Red, Yellow, brown and green,
Dot the landscape with a uniform order of perfection.
We travel to the mountains to explore the gift of Mother Nature

Nothing prepares us for the pastel of colors displayed on the trees.
The animals know it's almost time to go into hiding.
The cold front is slowly moving in and the deep beckons
The bear is ready for the yearly hibernation.
Forsaken for the long stupor ahead.

The trees have shed all to the barest essentials
I can see through the hillsides miles away.
All that was hidden is now in the open.

For the entire path it carved through our lives,
Irene made a Landfall that cost so much,
But in its wake is a new beginning within the landfill of life.
A new season begins with the advent of fall.
The attire of summer is retired for another year.

We admire and remember the adventures at the pool.
The endless trips to
Beach and the park.
It seems to be a distant memory with the landing of fall.
A reminder that life is but a circle that comes and goes.

## I Don't Want To

I don't want to eat,
I don't want to work
I don't want to go,
I don't want to nap.

I don't want to cry,
I don't want to go to bed.
I don't want to obey,
I don't want to drive.

I don't want to study,
I don't want to deliver.
I don't want to swim,
I don't want to dive.

I don't want to run,
I don't want to succeed
I don't want to fail,
I don't want to learn
If that is the case,
Then you don't want to flourish.

Life is not about choices in denial,
But about choices that leads to a well-fulfilled life
I can imagine that it takes a lot to move
To slide towards the goal
Of the marksman.

Flying and citing the goals that litter all around
Swaying to the sound of calypso in the soul
Ever prompting me to grab for the sky and hold the cloud
The witnesses that surround
The shadows of fortitude.

The spikes, piercing the softness of doubt
Never failing to leave a reminder that toil comes before the fame
He used to be me
He made a move and left the trail.

A choice to set aside the limitations of circumstances
The cover for those who seek but are just too meek
Figures are ever coming closer than I thought
In my head, I feel the roaster of the grind.

The toaster-spewing out slices of ideas
Left untouched, hardened and misplaced
I guide myself to the paths of the unforgotten
Noting that no matter the task, all it asks is the first step.

## I Tried to Let It Go

Times when my head was low.
It keeps getting faster but always slow
Each step heavier than the last.
I feast on the everlasting Grace.

Struggles and Pain sometimes is a staple.
We couple all our collective wisdom
Guiding and binding the glue that keeps us
No Matter how long it takes, I keep moving.

You really don't want to know
Where I've been or try to sow
I collect the sheets of Snow
Gathering by the corner of the Street.

It feels good when I realize,
The Passion born on the inside,
Feeding the multitude of thoughts and dreams
Culminating into a vision born from within.

## In Search of Peace

In search of peace I found war
Brokenness, pain and loneliness
In all, I lost it all.
Hope, laughter and joy
I searched in vain and I found nothing.

Under the crevices and behind stones
Heaviness weight and hopelessness
I tried but was tired
I looked but was overlooked
I tasted but was tested.

Over and over again
In search of peace
Till I found the Prince of peace.

## Is It Over?

It's not your fate.
There is nothing like 'I cannot make it'
Pull yourself up through the bootstraps.
You might feel weak, dejected and rejected.
But try.

Mistakes are bound to happen.
Nobody is immune to the deadly virus.
It latches to our thought system and replicates.
It stretches and takes hold.

I worry sometimes.
Things are not going right.
I faint at the pace of my progress.
Is it too late for me?

I will make it.
No Matter what I am going through.
I will rise above it.
Eagles sow above the rest.
Over temporary situations.

I am above and not beneath.
I will build on today's victory.
It's not over.
It's just the beginning.

# Iya Abiye of Igbajo-Land

My mum died Empty
She used all the talents and gifting,
Endowed by the Almighty.
She maximized her potential for the greatest good.

First as a child, wife, Mother, Nurse Practitioner and Educator,
To Principal of School of Midwifery U.C.H
An accomplished author and poet
A deaconess with the Nigerian Baptist
The Iya Abiye of Igbajo Land.

She laid markers that will guide many for years to come.
Accepting every challenge and leveling every mountain
Locking up 'No'
And adopting 'Yes' as her Mantra.
She created a path where there was none.
Forging ahead alone through winding roads and windy streams.

As life will have it, with the passage of time
Her strength slowly ebbed but she never gave up.
The medications were always present
And the Pharmacy were frequent visits
Come what may, She stood Tall.

There were days she tried to walk
Forgetting the half strength of her Knees
She tried despite the motion betrayal.
Her strength became faint and that is not fun
A body once strong showed signs of physical frailties.

There was a time she was strong and Healthy,
Running from Pillar to Post.
Striving and making a difference in a mutating world,
Laying markers for Humanity to review and record.
Her favorite anthem was 'Great is thy Faithfulness'.

The Holy Bible says
'I was once young and now I am Old,
I have never seen the righteous forsaken
Nor his seed beg for bread'.
Even in the farthest cave,
He will send a sparrow with a loaf for my sustenance.

Make hay while the Sun Shines.
Life is like an hourglass with a finite number of Sand.
For some, it's plentiful and gracious.
For others, it ends even before it begins.

I have heard people say that Life is unfair.
Who is the arbiter of the fairness quotient?
You, me?
Or the Man above?
It's a discussion that is best answered at the Pearly Gates.

For all the grave and perceived imperfections, I say thank you!
My Weakness is made perfect in your Strength.
When I am tired, you lift me up.
The fear of the Lord is the beginning of Wisdom.

## Jokilicious

She was born forty years ago
In the land of the free and the home of the brave
She weighed seven pounds and six ounces
Always smiling
And hardly crying.

Leading in everything she does
Helping others to always rejoice
When touched she simply recoils
Joke was always jovial and full of retort.

Elementary was at Staff school
Middle and high were at Fego
College was close to home at the University College
She loves nature and all its foliage.

She was always with three jolly friends
Lola, Yemisi and Enoma
To most they were known as the Pointer sisters
Full of virtue and hardly
Needing any assistance.

Then, she met this guy called Paul
At first he was Lucifer or Saul
Until she found a rare gem of affection
In his heart which truly ran deep.

Three sons after and hoping for more
Dele, Tobi and Femi begging for a sister
Every night she robs his gentle thighs
Saying 'lets try for just one more'
A girl that I can see and adore.

Peju, Bola, Bimpe and Titi
Her darling sisters just like Nerfertiti
The goddess of beauty in the ancient folktales
They all love drinks and cocktails.

Joke you are simply 'Jokilicious'
Full of Fun and bobbling with vigor
Her folks Dr and Mrs. Aina
Knew you will always be delicious.

To you we say Hip Hop Hurray
Hay Ho Hay Ho.

## Just Bloom

Once upon a time, I always complained
About all the reasons for lagging behind
Laying all the pain at the foothills of excuses
Such as doubts, others and destiny
Searching everywhere
Except the image in the mirror.

Always in thoughts and often depressed
I opined that the reasons were beyond my reach
Confidence slowly ebbed away and despondency set in
I starred a lot, wondered often, but never attained.

Giving into all the nay Sayers
I simply threw in the towel
The sky always looked dark
My talents were kept out of sight.

I reflected on the passage of time
Failing to realize the fault was mostly mine
Throwing away seeds and talents, dreams and plans
I looked the other way in search of the prize.

The seeds, talents, dreams and plans
Were the nuggets of the prizes I sought all along?
Then one faithful day I asked why?
It struck me that I never tried to harness the wind.

The opportunities lay bare and often overlooked
Relationships I never bothered to nurture
Where do I go from here and what do I do?

I will leverage my strength and vision
Throwing away the blame and blooming instead
I wake up my inalienable talents
The passions within me begin to boil

I channel the energy toward my objective.
I reminisce about the journey of the seed
Thrown into a hole and often forgotten
Covered up with earth,
Worms and the warmth of the sun
It dies and then it slowly blooms
Like the force of Nature,
It emerges after birthing pains and celebrating life.

In time, it blooms with vibrant colors
Lovely flowers and deeper roots
Beautifying the landscape with the splash of life
Turning a dying moment into a living moment.

The time for excuses is over
I choose to step out of my shell
Moving slowly toward the Tunnel of lights
Following the path laid toward my vision

No matter how long or the failed attempts
I do it over and over again
I fortify myself with a winning team
I search for the best and leave the rest.

We strive toward a common goal
Settling for nothing except Success
Arise, dust away the failures and bloom.

## Life in Seconds

Grains of sand in a bottle.
Turned upside down through a thing Opening.
It seeps continuously but never stops.
No matter how you try, it keeps emptying.

Life is not really promised.
We have a few seconds to live.
The only thing that matters is how
We spend those precious seconds.

It was just yesterday that I was born.
Crawling around the empty space.
Dependent for sustenance.
And Now, I am responsible for others that crawl.

The cycle of life is like a fast flowing river.
It keeps flowing no matter the obstacle.
Nothing stops it, nothing can.
Holding back and procrastinating
Wastes precious seconds.

Once it's out, it cannot be returned.
We cannot roll back the hands of time.
Regrets about yesterday and yesteryears are a waste.
Make the best of today coz life is in seconds.

## Little Steps

In all you do, try little bits
Tiny bits but try
In all you do, move little steps
Tiny steps but move
In all you do, sweat little drops.

Tiny drops but sweat
In all you do, pray little words
Tiny words but pray
In all you do climb little heights
Tiny heights, but climb.

It could be tough, sometimes-rough
Trying never hurts, a little here and there
Adds up to the mountain top
The best crop starts from a little seed
Planted and nurtured in love.

No matter how long it takes
Tick at it and tracks the ticks
Seconds will eventually add up to an hour.
Discovery is the art of recovery
By the seashore, all we do is pick shells.

Different shapes, but differing stories
They once lived, their story lives on
To be cherished and admired
We hope that after life we'll not be a shell
But a life full of vigor and vitality.

Never one under the Bushel.
I swing to the pangs of pain
the realities of disappointments
the reinforcement of a better future.
The magnificence of splendors to come

It might be a long way off
It will soon be a day off
Just a step away from the revered prize.

Life is fulfilled with trophies
the landscape is often dotted with folly
Just keep moving and giving
The winds will always be behind your wings
Arriving at destinations yet unknown.

To the right or the left
Backwards or forwards
the directions, really meets up to the path
Laced with prizes not yet claimed
Sometimes, I stand and stare and wonder
At the awesome power of movement.

## Love Speaks Louder than Words

Love my mind and my body
Love me for who I am
Love my intentions and my deeds
Love my plans and my visions.
I am open to love, if you are open to change.

Love is actions in motions
Love is more than words and seasonal actions
Love is an experience and a journey
It is a confluence of lives coming together as one.

Love sometimes hurts
It is the oil that ensures its posterity
No matter the challenge, love conquers all
You have the power to out- love your pains
For you to truly love, you have to love yourself.

The stream flows over the boulders and the ditches
Sometimes calm and often restless
It shines at the height of the midday Sun
It teems with life and offers serenity to others
Love is a stream that flows through the paths of life.

Your words are like sweet medicine to my soul
How long will it last?
Do you mean every single phrase?
Are they for now or eternity?
Do I need to inspect what I expect?
Love is only love when it has passed the test of time.
Love is at the end and not the beginning.

At times it towers like a mountain
Soaring into the sky and clouds
Featuring steep hills and slippery slopes.
Sparse vegetations or lush greenery
It takes a lot to get to the summit

Without care we fall and roll down the sides
Just like Jack and Jill up the Hill.
We need to remember
What it took to get to the mountaintop.

Love is a choice. We choose to love
It's not as simple as it seems
We often go against the school of thought
That say, the next step should be hate.
It's a commitment that stays
The course no matter the outcome.

Love breeds conflicts
The conflicts are the threads that make you stronger
Sometimes our minds are left with bitter memories.
We loose some and we loose most.
The grounds are littered with casualties of love.

Love speaks louder than words.
The honeymoon is over.
The sunlight has pierced the darkness of ignorance.
I loved with all I Had, and it still hurts
I gave you my all, my soul for keeps.

Your words were like the building blocks to my soul
They made my eyes twinkle like the stars,
Lightened up my day with a smile or laughter,
You had me twisted around your fingers.

You cannot love those that are incapable of love
They squander all the emotional gifts showered
They abuse physically and mentally
They turn the experience into a Nightmare
At that point I dream of me
The Love that endures, I choose to love me.
God is love now and always
He loved us just the way we are
Taking us with our baggage and concerns
Dying on the cross for you and me.

He had the power to destroy,
Yet he submitted at Calvary for the sake of Love.
When you truly love, look at the cross,
As the perfect symbol before you fall out of love.

## Luger Nodar Kumaritashvili

Final training day in Vancouver
A warm wet day holding lots of promise
Twenty-one and full of life and vigor
Totally in love with the blind alleys of the luge
It is my destiny to be a pilot.

Getting here was a long time coming
The stage set in the Eastern Bloc
Sliding down the slopes and around the block
Loosing count of the daily clock.

I lay flat in my favorite hiding place
My helmet is secure and belted in place
All I require is just a slight push
Here comes the awesome adrenaline rush.

The speeds are truly awesome
Corners and jerks really testy
I pierce the air, as I get feisty
A great time for fun and fiesta.

Am dizzy the turns are getting sharper
The speed is getting greater
The crowds are screaming louder
The challenge is simply unbelievable.

It's like climbing a mountain down hill
It could be smooth and uneventful
Or it could a wild avalanche
Threatening to bury and to take you with it.

I have seen and heard of people
Who took the first plunge,
But never came back?
Sometimes it's a cloud of witnesses
A maze of endless corridors.

## Our Love is Here to Stay

My love story has been a good story
The twists and turns have been filled with excitement.
Looking into my heart, I see the one I love,
Walking on the pink sands of Antigua and Barbuda.

Today, I celebrate you.
Through the twists and turns,
I never once imagined life with any other.

Thank you for Today and Yesterdays.
We took a vow of Commitment and trust.
Words fail sometimes to express how I feel.
You are still the Apple of my eyes.

Valentines Day is not just one day.
It's everyday for those that truly love.
Love is not a feeling that comes and goes.
It lingers through the darkest hours.

True love outlasts the struggles,
It wins every race life might bring.
We need to be grateful for what we have.
Our love is here to stay.

## Macabre Dance

I hear the African Drums
Piercing through the Night.
The Birds take to flight
At the sight of the Masquerade.
Adorned in a million colors
Swinging wildly to the rhythm
Everyone around in visible trepidation.

I climb walls in my head
I seek the voices of reason
I drop the lines of aspersion
I redeem the spirits that lie restless within me.

The spirits wake up and my eyes are like fire.
I speak the language of the great unknown.
I rise above the ground defying the forces of Gravity.
I swing like a pendulum in the Grandfather clock.

The leaves and the trees are aware of my presence.
They coil and hide themselves from the cataclysmic event
I embody the beginning of the festival of sticks
The Drums increase the intensity of the day.

It's not a spectacle.
It's a celebration of the bountiful harvest
The generosity of natures wonder
Planting a seed and reaping a plant.

How do the Yam cuttings buried in the ground,
Germinate into a vine adorned with green leaves?
How does the percolating water find its way to the roots?
Questions worthy of our celebration.

The very finest will be consumed today.
We roast the Yam on the Burning Fire.
Enjoying it with Palm kernels harvested the day before.
The squirrels hang around for an opportunity for leftovers.

The villagers join in the celebration.
Tomorrow, the Market will be full with Fruits and vegetables.
Money in the Pocket for industrious Farmers.
Arranging the produce on straight rows on the table.

The King arrives!
His entourage of chiefs walks briskly ahead of him.
They make way for the Royal One.
All the Villagers Lie prostrate on the ground
He waves his staff of authority at the Loyal Subjects.
May all of you last long on the face of the Earth?

May the produce of the year bring prosperity to the village?
May young and healthy children be born this year?
May we be protected from the wrath of nature?
May our joy not turn to sadness?
May the spear never pierce our side?
May we live long in the land of the living?

The Ladies and children join in the celebration
Singing and dancing wildly till Early Morning.
Stripping faces with white markings and coal
White and Black faces as far as the eye can see.

The macabre dance comes once in a year.
A time to let loose and give ourselves away
To the exceeding expectation from the Earth.

The masquerade slowly makes its way back to the Palace
A sign that the festival is almost over.
We rejoice at the rebirth of the Harvest.

# Mother Nile

From the beginning of time it has flowed
fertilizing the tributaries and the marshlands
the white and blue Nile flow for thousands of Miles
As long as it glows we will never be in denial of smiles.

It stretches through regions and races
when it overflows we brace up for long faces
Carving new paths and leaving lots of traces
A reminder that the Nile is really ageless and spotless.

The source of legends
The reasons for gods
'Ra' also known as the Sun god
'Hapi' the god of the upper and lower Nile
They looked up to them for bountiful harvests.

Cities sprung up all around it
The Luxor and Thebes just to mention a few
Bringing tourists from far and near
To the source of the Pyramids and Pharaohs.

The boats and the fishermen rely on it
The Salmon, Trout and crocodiles skate on it
The Aswan Dam is built right on it
Providing the Sun to many at dusk.

The reeds hid the biblical baby Moses
Handing the world the first paper called papyrus
Revealing tales from Ancient labyrinth
leading us into adventures through ancient monuments.

Tributaries and Estuaries flow from it
Forming water sources for villages and farms
Irrigating and mitigating the scourge of Famine
Providing a highway for ships from Asia Minor.

The circle of life is sustained because of the Nile
Where will Egypt be without the Nile?
Sudan and Ethiopia, Rwanda and Kenya?
All Lay claims to the abundance of the mighty river.

Mother Nile has many siblings
Amenhotep III, Cleopatra, and Tutankhamun
Reigned in majesty and left a mark
The tombs bear tales of their great riches
Laid at the sacred sites of the Mummies
The Nile is Egypt and Egypt is the Nile.

## Mountains

All shapes and sizes.
Rough, smooth, jagged and rough.
Orographic and Leeward.
The windward side picks up wind.

It towers far above the horizon.
Rising with Majesty into the sky.
The summit displays snow at the cap.
Weathering reveals cracks and grooves.

The Mountain spoke.
'I am here to stay'
'I am firmly rooted and will go nowhere'
'I am a force to reckon with'
Don't you know me?
'I am the rock on your way'.

I stop and stare.
Imposing and Majestic!
Towering over my strength and abilities.
There is no way I can climb.

Do I try to climb to the very top?
Do I just walk around the waistline?
Do I blow a hole through the mountain?
Or do I just speak?

I choose to speak.
Words of encouragement and faith.
I speak to every mountain.
It's not real,
It will not stay.

# Moyosola

The smiles are unimaginable
The crackles brings joy to every heart
The cute little face makes the sun shine brighter
To have and to behold the red dress speaks volumes.

The eyes are deep but bright
The ears are eager to listen and learn
The uncharted territories the tame seas
The tabula rasa an eternity awaits
Who is she?
Her name is Moyosola.

# My Favorite Blanket

Why bother to lay it over
The princess still sleeps in it now that she's older
Without her blanket, she soon discovers
She sheds sweats and thirsts
For the calmness it provides in her mind.

Mirroring the colors of the rainbow
Patches of textures sewn together in unison
The devotion from Grandma became my garrison
 As I held it in my arms tears of joy was clearly visible.

It's woven in love and memories
She's addicted to every corner of the tapestry
Although worn, the blanket makes her airborne
The journey it took is far and wide
Through planes, trains and Buses
Tucked in suitcases packed for the summer get- away.

It has some holes but is okay
It's smaller but is not a bother
The blanket has been used for years
 All the memories are badges of honor.

I got it when I was three
I still have it now that I am Twenty -three
Without it my sleep is long drawn and crowded
Figures with bulgy eyes and funny shapes.

I love it so much I named it 'Chaps'.
Mostly been the subject of dreams
She beams and I hide in a forte
Her tapestry was woven in love and fright.

Each thread lay with painstaking care and attention
It provided a much-needed shield
From the frequent frightening lightning strikes
Illuminating the bright summer blue sky.

My Blanket has Eyes.
Every strike encourages me to pull tighter.
During several strange and boisterous thunder storms
At times I wish you were my magic carpet
Flying through distant lands in a lovely basket.

I thrive in memories that linger
Rubbing my skin against the pillows of Alaska
The ice is melting and the weather is changing
Each thread is a mark of assurance
Closely monitoring the edges of the breakthrough.

The minutes are adding up to the days foretold
Wonders yet to be discovered often imagined
I sleep and the cover is slowly falling
The chill of the night wakes me.

I stretch; I grab my friend and slowly pull it close
The size envelope me with a warm embrace
I snooze through the dark calls of the night.
Sweet dreams my fair lady, Goodnight.

# Mayowa

Mayowa is the first and what a Joy!
Her Nickname is Sunshine and don't you forget.
A Chinese baby she was called at birth
Her complexion was as the color of the snow.

Full of energy and that is no joke
Smiling, dining and whining,
Mayowa is gracious and always proper.
Asking numerous times, what's for Supper?

On the fifteenth day she arrived
Announcing in the Month of may
With His Grace, I am here to stay
I love you so much and that is my mainstay.

Growing up to be a lovely damsel,
Learning so much along the way.
I wonder what lies ahead of you
Everything you touch is so cool.

If you ask her, she'll always say,
'I love my Family' that's for sure.
A spoon in the pot to save a trip
Reading slowly and gently from the script.

## Ode to Forty

The day finally came when the clock struck forty
A mild day full of thoughts about the life that lay ahead
I stared at myself in the mirror
A mirage of contrasting Images collide with sorrow.

I salute the bravery of birth
Grinding through the furnace of time
linking my steps through the maze of reality
I march toward the Appalachian horizon.

What happened to the dreams I had?
The visions I held dear?
The goals unshakable and clearly discernible
Objectives I wrote down and clearly believed.

The hour- glass appears
The scale clearly tilts in the balance
An hour full or an hour empty?
Does life truly begin at forty?

Longing to rationalize the reality of existence
Accepting that the best is yet to come
I lean toward the podium of ages
Anxious for an opportunity to dance on stage.

I was once young, now I feel younger
Dreading the journey that must be taken
Grasping at the enormity of the task that lie ahead
Like the grasshopper, I perch and with limbs akimbo I wait
My destiny slowly completes its metamorphosis.

The marksman in me has the aim in the brush ears
All the game in the forest heading toward the quiet streams
One good shot and life converges

Those that always jeered are bound to marvel
At the perfection of the marksman's range.
Twinkled and now the stars
I often wonder when my lot will change
We worry often about life's little tricks
Rocking on the chair that comforts but never resolves.

At forty, it's either north or South
Having the courage to own the outcome
I take the steps with a determined ease
Waking up the roar that lies within.

My bulk wood chest is full of goods
That seem to have lost its meaning.
The trophies appear dull and lackluster
In retrospect, my mistakes and failures are fuel for my future.

I choose to lead through service
Helping those I have never known
Lifting the souls of those that are the outcast of the town
Accepting no glory for those that were once the village clown.

At forty, I choose to celebrate
The gift of life that is so dear
A promise that is so rare
The wine seems sweeter as it ages
Heeding the clear warning of the sages.
Alas I dash through the tape of forty.

## Oil Spill in the Gulf

It comes in waves
Just bits now and then
The soil is soaked in silt
It's slowly killing what we built.

I try to cry but no
All I know is almost gone
Our defense is sure to break
The little we did is soaked away.

It gets into holes
The sands can't stand its coat
The blob is over the sand
The finest are prey to the dance.

By the day we slowly perish
Our source of food in the parish
Is lying waste on the horizon
The Bands and music are slowing ebbing
Coz the people are almost gone.

The Bills are sky high
On our knees we pick tar balls
We skim and skim and skim
The more we try the more we see
The oil and it makes us boil.

The booms and the boats
The spades and the shovels
The masks and the coats
The shoes and the gloves.

The dispersants and the inhabitants
All seem to dance to the macabre dance
Strange partners best of friends.
We used to smile; now it's been a while.

We while away the time by swallowing our bile
Bitter, but sweet we've lost the taste for tweets
The birds used to dive
But now they dive to their graves.

Soaked in oil and covered in foil
They try to fly, but can only stand and coil
The reds and Blues shout and scream
They point figures and blame all but the sky.

It's funny to stand and watch the theater
While most loose all now and after
The caps, the hoses, the ships and the relief wells
All we pray for is just some relief
From the agony that now seems so normal.

I don't need the money
Don't try to be a phony
Just leave me with my bologna
The gulf was my source
You made it all of a sudden a curse.

# The Queen of Oprah

Her name is Oprah.
She is faster than a Toyota Supra
Name it and she has done it
Always willing to break down all barriers
With the Universal gift of Knowledge.

Her words hits the right cord
In her, there is truly no discord
Sometimes she chooses to fly in a Concord
To everybody that asks, she gives an umbilical cord.

She is strong; in her weakness she is stronger
From humble backgrounds with just a little ginger
She looks back and sees a foundation of fonder
Propelling her to become one of the greatest harbingers.

You know she is the queen of Opera
In all her acts, she makes a mark
Her school trains for life
Builds little babes into bed-rocks
Forming the cornerstone of a firm building.

Compassion is always second nature
The Queen always tries to nurture
For every broken heart, she has a suture
Bring it on because she can take the torture.

Teary eyed for the pain of others
Touching, feeling, and always seeing
Every single day she gives her very best
To every person she meets, she blesses.
What a woman, what a life.

She has touched so much
Done so much
Given so much
Being through so much
She makes every thing she touches grow
You can refer to her as Oprah-Mulch.

She writes in the 'O'
She models and appears on the Cover
So beautiful, she defies the ages
All you have to do is go through the pages
Of a life spent in the pursuit of a purpose
To pour all she could I suppose?

To Oprah, you will be truly missed
Thank you for all you have done
And all the brilliant pastels you've painted
You will always be the Queen of Oprah.

# Rachel

Young wise and vibrant
Virtuous, tender and so bright
An only child, a miracle Child
Born out of adversity ever so mild
Sent to Minna, when only a Minor
To be taught and brought up on a manor.

A teacher she became
At Idi-Aba was the Sesame
That opened the door to the globe
The world became smaller as she strode.

The corridors of learning
May Perry was her favorite
A teacher of exceptional character
Hailed from Canton Georgia.

To Africa obeying the savior
Laying a mark always to be savored
What a mission, what a missionary
She was Hannah and not ordinary.

At Baba Lawoyin she met Isaac
Love at first sight at the site
Swept off her feet and away on the kite
Married with seven golden children.
Through struggle, pain and sacrifice
The seven all stood on a sure foundation
Of Christ which is our inheritance.

She could have left
But she stayed
For the seven she gave it all
Walked on fire, coal and dust
She endured all the frost that bites
And leaves everlasting marks.

Now frail but the less no tail
She's still the head in all she does
Walks with a Cain but still keen
About knowledge with a pen
Inspiring others to do the same.

Memories of Rachel are fresh
Piles of it are stored in our minds
She gave and still gives
All she has and ever had.

Herself!!!!!!
That's all we ask
That's all we need
And it's more than enough.

## Remove the Training Wheels

Remove the training wheels
Fall if you may but rise you must
The time to forsake childish ways have come
Fearful because of all that lie ahead
I wish away the past and usher in the future.

I take the first step in fright
I practice all I was taught and brace myself
The inevitable happens and I take a plunge
The support I once had and relished is gone.

Where do I start?
How do I cope and what lies ahead?
Nobody knows not even I.
I lie on the floor and soak the moment.

The supplies I had were endless
Others laid their lives on the line instead of mine
The news was my staple for those that laid it all
Now the time has come for me to shed some weight.

We were a loose confederation of fiefdoms
There were no kings and the land was bare
The strongest wielded the might
The sword was the arbiter for peace.

I saw men of great estate bleed on the fields of Battle
Foreign as they were, they still believed in Nationhood
They built schools, Hospitals and Bridges
They built roads, homes and Airports
For their effort we lay mines and explosives.

I wonder why they came
some so young and naive
barely strong enough to lift their bag packs
they walked with us and kept going
No matter the cost.

For years they were right there by our side
Taking the first brunt of every attack
Shielding us from the wave of terror
I duff my hat to these Men and Women and say thank you.

The training wheels are off and suddenly we feel a cloud
Stranger than most settling over the horizon
Our blood have been spill in the water
The sharks smell blood and are swimming for the kill
We abandon our post and take cover.

Suddenly there was confusion all over
Men were dropping like flies
Friends, cousins and fellow soldiers
All fell at the erratic music of Bullets
The days of reckoning are here.

During the pandemonium that broke
We suddenly realized that we had to turn
Towards the hail and fire of terror
We need to want it more than most
It was after all our Motherland.

Bleed we may, but fight we must
Our Flag must not fall to the invaders of our faith
Camouflaging their atrocities in the guise of religion
Our fertile lands still holds the bones of our Ancestors.

We are steadfast and stand together at the gates
The game we lost just began.
Our Freedom must not be lost.
Stand now and be counted for the quest for peace.

# Secret Chambers of the Heart

It's bitter sweet
A taste of Ice tea
The touch felt like the dew of the early morn
I dreamt about this for so long
The night I hold so tight I hardly want to let go.

I know I should, but something says no
I move slowly, but my mind says so
I look closely and I see eyes as cool as the Sea
The next move tells me I should lie in the sea breeze.

I read the words and it feels so lovely
Every word sends a sudden volley
Through my spine and aching heart
I accept the loneliness of my thoughts
The emptiness of my sighs.

Love should be fun
Sometimes I feel I should just take off and run
I take little steps and hope for massive leaps
Heaps abound everywhere of mounds unsettled.

Words are beautiful but could be laced with poison
Sounding great and meaning so little
Always attached to an ulterior motive
Never truly meaning what it professes.

It could be the best day of my life
The one memory I refuse to let go
The act that makes life worth leaving
Imaginations running wild, but beautifully crafted.

It's a mosaic of wild colors
It's the aphrodisiac that slowly spreads a message
Not a rush of fools as some may believe
A rainbow of shining lights under our sleeves.

I am in a race
The lace of the ropes of love
The noose close to my neck
Despite the reassurance that it's just a nectar
It suddenly tastes like bile.
I thought love was simply a land of Jive.

## Segun Sege

Immaculate, Determined with fortitude.
A man that leads and others simply follow.
Shy and resolute and cool as the Bahamas Breeze
He strides along a passionate path.
He's tall and handsome and hardly needs an introduction.

A couple of years ago, I had a friend named Segun,
He was equally calm and collected and we had a song for Him.
He hated it, but it was fuel for us to sing it even louder.
'Segun sege, Omo Mamae'!
It simply means Segun, the favorite son of his mother.

It holds true for the kind soul we celebrate today.
He puts God first in everything he does.
Commit your ways unto the Lord, Acknowledge Him
In all your ways and He will make your way prosperous.

Intelligent, smart and articulate.
He enunciates his words with ease and clarity.
Ask Segun and he knows about most subjects
Arts, Politics, Sports, Medicine, Greek Mythology,
Lord of the rings, Food, and most especially Abbey.

He holds her dear, leaving a trail of roses on her path.
He cherishes her and whispers kind words in her ears.
Going for Long walks and endless conversations on the phone.
It was a match in heaven ordained on earth.

He's a jolly good fellow and he deserves a toast.
Good taste, Fashionable, Cute and adorable.
From Corona, to Ijanikin, to the University college.
He was always at the top of his class.

Today is a day set apart for you Segun.
We all love you so dearly because of whom you are.
Kind and always the perfect gentleman in all you do.
It brings me back to my favorite song for my friend.

Segun Sege, Omo Mamae.
Happy Birthday dude,
But Remember that Man City Won.

## Split Personality

I will be a Pilot in two weeks
I will write the next best seller in a Month
I intend to travel to the moon on the Midnight Express
I feel I can jump over the Mount called Everest
I can swim across the Pacific Ocean.

I am training to be a fire fighter.
A lawyer is my true calling.
If I wanted, I could be the next Olympiad.
Farming really comes easy to me.

To a few I need some Meds
To quiet the thoughts and the Visions
That takes me round the Eiffel tower
And quiet the voices of the hour.

They just don't know me
I am smarter than the nuclear scientist
Just let the right opportunity swing my way
I can break the Enigma code.
I invented the highway called the Internet.

There are a few things to ask
Why is the world so tough?
Why do the children seek and never find?
Why are the Innocent ones out of luck?
Why do I sit here as a lame duck?

I know what to do.
The stars will lead me on my way
To Mama Clara up in the hills
For a quick look at the palm of my hands
Left or right, she is bound to reveal.
Don't you dare push me?
I will fall if you do

Over the edge to the lowest valley
Shattering into a million pieces
Appearing in the dreams of many.

I try to sleep, at the toil of the day
I reap the sounds of the Unicorn
I take a bite out of the cooked yellow corn
Lying fallow beneath the fields just sown.

The day is night and the night is day
I sprint towards the waterfalls
Just ahead towards the bend
I taste the sight of the Pentecost
A baptism in remembrance of renewal.

I dance wildly at the idea of freedom
The drums of rainbow beyond the horizon
Down towards the great beyond
The silence is really deafening
Speak to the voices and make them disappear.

# Summer Breeze

The snow has melted.
The brown leaves are green again!
The Birds have begun to fly and sing sweet tones,
My mind is imagining again,
It's time for the Summer Breeze.

I feel the heat and the wind have lost its cool.
The kids and the neighborhood pets are out of school.
The additions and subtractions are long forgotten,
The History lessons are all begotten.
I try to remember but I have a brain freeze.

I step outside for a while,
The heat is unkind to my hide.
The children are indoors playing hide and seek,
Grown-ups are silently sipping a cold shake.

The fourth of July is around the corner
The grill is washed and dried by the owner
Fish, corn, steak and Lamb chops are
Seasoned with salt, spices and Onions,
The oil slowly drains from the tired Fat
Hunger pangs increase as I Adjust my Hat.

The lawn is green and lush.
My Mower slowly roars back to life:
I survey the yard with painstaking alarm!
The weeds beg for mercy to no avail.
It's time for weekly grass haircut.

The creek is drying up!
The farmer knows that without rain,
His crops will wither and fail:
His countenance is Crooked and frail,
The only hope is the erratic Thunderstorm.

Summer Camps are busy again,
The staff has to keep up the Tempo,
Fieldtrips to the Zoo and the Fire stations
 Slowly translates into stories with summer legs.

The Sun shines down beautifully,
The Glow is all but magical
How could something so far away?
Have such wonderful summer breeze?
I beam and smile and my worries sleep.
As I remind myself it's just the annual summer breeze.

# Superwoman's Creed

I am a superwoman by choice
My choice is to save my kids and I
From roads that seem endless
The shine has lost the luster
I face my lot and remain a hustler.

Four babies after all said and done
And all she got from him was exactly none
She picked so much bone
The plan was for the best of time
Instead she got was the worst of time.

She dusted herself and laced her boots
Like the phoenix she rose
One brick at a time
A good foundation for the kids she laid.

Her body bears the mark
Several nights crying to sleep
Wondering why the hills are so steep
Every step I make I seem to slip.

I am a woman.
My veins liven up with possibilities
Sweating to make a home I can call my own
I set my eyes on the future, not the past.

The seas are rough, so am I
I jump in despite the tempest
The rising waves take me higher and further
Proving that I can still make a home without a father.

Waking up at four and sleeping at eleven
Setting the table with bagels and scrambled eggs
The school Bus always leaves at seven
Pre-school closes at the tip of two.

I am full of energy
I prod myself towards waves of destiny
The tornados take me to unknown destination
There will be a day for a full restitution.

# Texting and Driving

I slammed on my brakes.
The pavement was scared.
I sweated and waved.
I just escaped by the whiskers.

Earlier, my phone buzzed.
Eyes off the steering for a second.
Quick look around and
I assured myself, all was well.

Quick glance at the message,
Looked up quickly and
In the split of a second
That it was safe to reply.

It will be short and sweet.
Before you know it.
It will be over and done with.
I started typing slowly but surely.

All it took was just a second.
My eyes was off the flow of traffic
Before I Knew it, I swerved, looked up and panicked.
My car was headed in the wrong direction.

I tried to recover.
The vehicle to my left was dangerously close.
My life flashed before my eyes and
Before I formed the next thought
I was in the ditch, and flipped.

After the shock, wore off.
I asked myself a simple question.
'Was it worth the risk'?
All for a text?

## The Ayo-Bello Legacy

How do you eulogize Dr Ayodeji Bello?
That achieved so much within a relatively short time?
How do you say Goodbye to an officer and a Gentleman?
How do you say Thank you for the wonderful memories?

Kindness and grace exhibited by a warm soul.
In our minds, the wound is fresh and it hurts,
But we accept that it is well with our soul.
Over Six Decades on the stage of Life making
Significant impact on the footprints of life.

A father to four wonderful children.
Muyiwa, the first and a physician healing the mind.
Buki, the second and a physician healing the eyes.
Mayowa, the third, an Engineer,
Fixing and developing great inventions.
Ayotunde, the fourth, a physician freshly minted.

A husband to Christy, Yetunde Ayo-Bello.
Loving, nurturing and partnering with his better half.
Endured in sickness and in health,
In want and in plenty
Loving to the very end.

A Brother to the Ayo-Bello Family.
A Patriarch who kept the Flag Flying for so long.
Building on the Legacy of Papa Rev Bello of the Nigerian Baptist,
A humble servant in the Household of Faith
Serving many years and leaving goodwill that knows no bounds.

To Toyin the Only Brother
To Kemi, Ike and Funke my lovely sisters,
I say, weep not for me.
My love for you will always abide.

He achieved so much in his lifetime.
Ayo Bello memorial Hospital.
Ayo Bello Foundation.
Alpha Hotels and Banquet hall
Touching lives and building Bridges.

He loved Kwara State so much.
Sole Administrator of the Sports Council,
Chairman of Kwara Bombers just to mention a few.
He never wanted to settle anywhere else but at home
Laying the foundations for future generations.

His passing is a void difficult to fill.
With God all things are possible and
He gives grace to the Humble.
He is at a place of peace, love and no sorrow.
Sipping Coffee with the Lord at the Pearly gates.

Personally, I miss you.
I remember the magic shows when I was 4 years Old.
Ring Bearer at your wedding at 8.
Your smile, encouraging words and frequent visits.

Our visit to the CNN Center,
Martin Luther King Memorial
And Stone Mountain Georgia.
The taproot of your love casts deep.

An awesome Brother and Son in Law.
You were present at most occasions and supportive.
Always calm like the Gentle seas
And Solid like the Rock of Gibraltar.
The Babalola's here and in the Diaspora
Are glad you were in our lives.
We will miss you greatly.

The essence of Life is not in the accumulation of wealth.
It's the Memories created and Life's touched.
You brought sight to the under-privileged.
Your smile is bright enough to light up a dark room.

The last text you sent to me read,
'Children are watching, never give up'
It will always be my Mantra
We will all miss you
As you rest in Gods perfect Bosom.

# The Best of Times, the Worst of Times

I tried so hard, but fell just before the reach.
I reached for the Top, but I found myself on the beach,
I teach the young, but I discover am still in Search,
I catch some air, but as I took a step, I fell into a ditch.

I scratch my head; but felt a stitch,
I thought my name was Ted, I soon realized I was fetch,
I brace for the fall, but the height left me in a daze,
The maze was huge and narrow, the trip just a phase,
The mouse was smart, but someone had stolen the Cheese.

The Night was dark, but the owls was up in the chill,
The morn was wet, in the mist of the early Frill,
In time I became the best, but it was at a price,
The figure skater pays for the slice,
Of the Ice she rolls on a dice.

The kite was high, but the rope was slim,
The air was tight, movement to the extreme,
The cream is sweet, but you feel the scream
I tried my best, but it wasn't good enough,
At best I was just short of the victory cough.

I could have, should have and might have
Bottles half full or half empty,
Never quite as much, always the same thing,
Through it all I got to the end of the maze,
Bumpy, made me feel like humpty dumpy,
Except there was no Great Fall.

The Men and the horses waited,
But I sat on the fence unabated
It took a while,
But here I am at the Promised Land.

## The Green Grass

It's everywhere,
It's the source of legends
It's the color of the rainbow
It feeds and it breeds
It takes one to make a million.

It travels to unknown destination
It stands erect and bows to the wind
Its soft but its strong
It's learnt to wave through the fury of the wind.

It's green or it's brown
It's purple or sometimes gold
It holds the sands in place
It smells fresh when in place.

Cows and goats know it all too well
And we know it too
We feed on the feeder
To others its just more fodder.

It covers the entire fields
Leave it for awhile and it cover it all
It provides cover for the small beings
And in time big beings bow to it.

Paintings that have it are lit
Landscapes come alive in all bits
Streams explode in an array of colors
It's the grass, the ever-present grass.

It is the very essence of the food chain
It feeds the cattle and the cattle feed us
When it's all said and done we feed the grass.
It never complains about the burden it bears.

The green pigment chlorophyll runs through its veins
It supplies the juices while holding the reins
Of the sun than shines through photosynthesis and rain
It magnifies and amplifies the growth of the mighty grass.

You see it through the glass cloud all across the plateau
Gentle and the source of joy to many
 It comes in different shapes and sizes
In all it does, it always entices.

Through the lushness of it's feel and colors
More comfortable than the beds of the Tudors
It sends its love everywhere it can
All across the land and through the mines.

Appearing in road cracks without a fine
Never truly knowing when to draw the line.
The green grass.

# The Hark and the Heralds

The heralds are singing
The birth of our savior is here
Born in a Manger for you and I
Lowly lying with the sheep and hay.

The kings brought gifts
To the King of Kings
Reigning Supreme in our lives
Living in our hearts and soul.

Once in a year we celebrate
Something special, unique and pure
An event more than a Thousand Old
The gift of a savior gentle and pure.

He was foretold in the book of the prophets
Announced by the angels who knew the way
Blessed to save and heal before he was born
Set apart for special times like these!

Mary and Joseph Knew of him
How could He be if we never knew each other?
Courted to marry, the marriage was still afar
Is He a source of joy or everlasting Joy?

Gifts are everywhere stacked to the sky
The seas glitter with the Christmas lights
The mood is proof of the event ahead
The birth of our savior Jesus Christ.

Is he the Gift or the source of all Gifts?
Is He the Giver or the Given?
Does he give to get or get to give?
He is the giver and source of all we know.

A Son of God sent for a cause
To rid us of all our sin and shame
A bridge across the gulf of sin
Separating us from the love of the father.

In the midst of the shopping
Stop to ask what it is all about?
Is it really Santa or the heavenly Santa?
That made the season so special and gracious.

The kids are excited about the visit from the North
The Poles are cold and the snow is falling
The nuts are slowly roasting on the fire and cracking
The gifts are wrapped and under the Christmas tree.

How about the gift He wrapped and gave to you?
The gift of healing and health
The gift of Miracles yet unknown
The gift of the breath of Life
The gift of the knowledge of his wisdom and love.

As we bundle up and race the cards
Do we care to give to the Poor?
A smile or a dollar to spare?
Ask yourself if you really have something to spare.

Celebrate him daily
Every second minute and hour
In every thing you do and say
Your life should be a song of praise
To the king who rules and reigns.

The jingle bells are ringing
A most wonderful time of the year
It's not about the gift, but the giver of all gifts
Jesus Christ our Lord and Savior.
Happy birthday to you.
Happy birthday to you in me.
Merry Christmas.

## A Heart of Stone

The hurt I feel is indescribable.
Unreachable and sometimes laughable.
Comical, magical and yet painful.
I lie awake, staring into the midnight sky.

I don't want to forgive.
The act of forgiveness is more painful.
It's easier to brew over the past and
Let it sit and fester
Boil over, spew over and burn the sidelines
All I feel is pain.

There was a time I believed in love.
I gave in the name of love.
Stooped in the name of love.
Denied in the name of love.
Forgave and forgot in the name of love.

Now it's a new heart order.
An eye for an eye and a tooth for a tooth.
For every heartache and pain,
I shell out three in return.
It might not be fun, but it is fair.

For a long time, I was your footstool.
You stepped all over me like a doormat.
I took it in stride,
But you never stopped.

There were several nights that I cried.
I begged you to stop.
You laughed and mocked
Saying, I had no clue.

I threw in the towel.
Waved a white flag.
You took it and burnt it.
Gathered the ashes and disposed it.
I took all the disrespect for the kids.
Innocent ones we are responsible for.
They did not ask to be born.
They were by us and now we teach them the cycle of pain.

The pain and the wounds inflicted are not on us.
It's on them.
They are molded by our actions.
It's not what we say, but what we do.

They will repeat what we do.
And so the story goes.
The generation passes the torch
Of the heart of pain.

# The Kiln of Purification

Walking through a field of burning Coal
Trying to get the whale out of the fish bowl
Bowing to the powers of the stormy Sea
Tying the noose against my hardened thighs.

The road I thread seems to be getting longer
The miles and hills getting steeper as I wonder
The mule I ride sliding as it steps up the mountain path
Breathing heavier seems to be my staple course.

The fire seems to be a constant companion
The ambers seething as the air blows along
The breeze is hot and mostly discomforting
The climb parallel against the course of traffic.

The more I try, the less I move
I feel like the road is littered with mud piles
The paths seems to be at cross roads
I pick up speed and hit a brick wall.

The stream erodes all the banks and ferns
The fishes on the banks expose their gills and fins
Trash flows wildly full of canteens
Once consumed by Cowboys wearing Bandanas.

I always thought I was alone
Chatting my course as I go along
Feeling all the heat that is just a feet long
Wondering if I will ever belong.

All the while, I have had help
At every turn and curve
The support I got kept me going
The loss I thought was gain after all.

In hindsight all the headaches
Were simply aches of wisdom?
Knocking on my door and window seal
The cold never came in because he was my heel
Helping me to keep my troubles at bay.

My troubles are my badges of honor
Shining through the horrors of Sodom
The piles of salt are moments of Victory
Assuring me of the upcoming Glory.
Gold becomes through the kiln of purification.

## The Leaks of Wiki

The annals are full.
Intimate details whispered in the dark,
Sip through the lips of the populace,
Ideas born in the minds of delegate.
Saturate in the Modern hemisphere.

Demonstrating the power of preservation.
The independence of the airwaves,
Dishes of the universal media,
Comments adorn the storage spaces.
Analyzed at the whims of the perpetrators.

How did it leak despite the containment?
Caged secrets reserved for the very few.
Carefully preserved for the consumption of the elite,
Explosive and divisive to the populace.
Spread through the bullhorns of Wiki.

The truth is an incandescent light bulb.
Once switched on, forever banishes the darkness.
Distorting the images carefully crafted for the herds.
Seeking guidance through the maze of oblivion.
The days of reckoning are near.

It will have an irreversible effect.
The Globe will forever be distorted,
Boundary lines have shifted,
and History is in need of a revision.
To some, it is a treasure trove of knowledge.

Accurate in detail and expansive in scope.
Shedding the beam of truth once and for all.
Giving credence to a lot of suspicion.
Or the self-centered dissemination to many,
Raw in detail and lacking logical truth.

So many people could be harmed.
The knowledge could implode kingdoms.
The corridors of power are weakened by revelations.
Ammunition to revolutionist around the globe.
We seek nothing more than the truth.

The whole truth and nothing but the truth.
Guiding our fickle minds and mangled wisdom,
wondering why the snail's speeds faster than it should.
It used to be summer, now its spring,
The seeds are germinating and News flourishes.

Temptations are lurking on every mind.
Whatever the cost, obscurity is lost.
A new age dawns at the acquittal of the first.
You wonder if we can really stand the truth.
Only time will tell as the hourglass empties.
The forest hides the creatures within.

## The Love That Once Was

They said it would last forever.
A match made in heaven.
Our personalities reminiscent of the story of Cupid
It happened to be a big bubble pricked by the reality of time.

I can love.
I have the capacity to love.
I want to be loved, held and appreciated.
To love is to be loved.
For you to love, you have to give.

Who are you?
What have you become?
What did I do?
Who is to blame?
You stood taller than the Empire State building
The majesty of your presence was a wonder to behold.

There was a time I was your sweetest Rose.
The One who makes your heart skip a beat.
The one who made your eyes twinkle with excitement?
I was the most beautiful woman on the Planet.

The one who moved to the sound of music,
The lady whose smile was like the Sun,
I was your comforter,
I was your friend.

I was the one you were devoted to,
I was joined to you at the Hip.
I was the second half of your heart.
You were the mighty one in my eyes.

You were so innocent,
You could do no wrong.
You were patient and Kind,
Your touch was softer than the softest pillow,
You hug like you were my protector,
You words made my head spin in cycles.

You knew it and you teased me.
You reached into the very depth of my heart.
You ripped it apart
With the words that were once magical.
Where has the love gone?
Our Love could still burn; it is never late to love.

We need to remember
The promises we made to each other.
We need to submit to each other
As sacrificial lambs to the altar.

Wake up from your slumber
And fan the embers of Love.
The rainbow that once delighted
Turned into a whirlwind of destruction
Breaking all the bricks of love
That once stood at the corner lot of my heart.

## The Making of a Mother

I saw you transform before my eyes.
Sleepless nights and Countless sacrifices
For the ones you love and those you hold dear.
You are so sweet and gentle and now that am grown,
I have come full circle in noting and appreciating,
We witnessed in amazement the extent of your selfless love.

You spent years on bended knees it seems,
Praying and waiting on the Lord for the same request,
Unwavering in your quest and unashamed in your zeal.
I wondered sometimes, if you'll call it a day and give up.
Instead, I saw the fervor of your steam engine roar stronger
Heading toward a safe destination for your Children.

It was not always easy at the place you called home.
You mothered all the children, both young and Old.
Somehow, you steered us all away from the pitfalls,
Shepherding us away from the Hungry Lions roaming in the wild.
At times we were lost, but your firm and gentle hands found a way.

There is no way, I can forget you sweet mother.
You will always be the star that shines brightest in the midnight sky
My memories of the pearls of wisdom still guide me today,
Fear the Lord, Love always, strive the hardest and keep a good name.
It's much better than silver or gold.

I love you so much dear mother.
Your blood flows within my veins and it moves me.
You bought less, so we could have more.
The nest you built still remains in our heart today,
It wasn't built out of brick or wood but love and devotion.

You never seemed to grow tired of us.
Everyday offered a new challenge, which you took in stride

If I was sick, you were there with medicine in hand and a kind heart
Your touch and voice was better than the best physician
The aroma of your presence nurtured me back to health.
It wasn't always easy in the place we called home.
I heard quarrels and arguments behind the door
There were times when we did not have enough,
With your magic touch, we seldom went to sleep hungry.

Coping sometimes with the death of a loved one.
Through it all, I saw you transform into a beautiful rose.
Words cannot describe today the love I Have for you.
Money cannot replace or repay the sacrifice you gave.
Although I reside in a far away land.

Your voice rings true everyday whispering ever so gently,
'Fear the Lord, run away from what is evil and a good name,
Is better than silver or gold'.
I love you Mama, you will always be the Queen of my heart.

# The Man Stored Within

I pull you out of the deep recesses.
The full potential of what you are meant to be.
I demand the fulfillment of your destiny.

The dreams I had of you are true.
It rings true to my soul and I laugh.
I marinate over the essence of your Manhood.

You are getting to the top of the mountain
You don't belong with the ants of the valley
Arise and shine as the new day dawns.

I search deep within you and I see
The softness that hides behind the muscle
The smile that hides behind the frown.

The plans I have for you are great
I can't force you my dear,
But I choose to encourage you.

You are my Husband, the father of my children
You are the one that brought out the best in me.
You are my friend and soul mate.

I spread my wings and fly with you,
To unknown destinations
Seeking nothing in return.

I wish you all of life's goodness
No matter the present circumstances
I see you cross the rivers of your troubles.

Love is what I felt the first time we met
Love is the motivation of my emotions
Love is not just the feeling but also the actions.

How do I say those words that mean so much?
Tied at the tip of my lips.
I surrender myself to you my dear
And wish you a happy father's day!

# The March into Greatness

There is a shadow behind me.
The past that hovers and clouds my horizon.
Resolutions I made in times past.
At the beginning of a new year.

There is nothing sweeter than the sounds of spring
The winter is ebbing and the sky is beautiful.
The grass slowly changes from the colors of brass to luscious green
Hibernation slowly comes to an end
The time to plant new seeds has come.

A time for the greatest beginning.
A time to pause and march into the vacuum of greatness
To chase the dreams of my collective destiny
I dive into the abyss of faith
I alight into the vision of a new dawn.

Out with the old and in with the new.
I change my attire and free myself of the collective weight
My elbows are free to express the enterprise I hold dear.
The invention in me screams for a natural birth
The pain might be great but the joy knows no bounds
Ideas freely expressed, naturally conceived.

The might within my soul has arisen
I rise to catch the silver lining in my cloud
I have been to the Mountaintop
I dear not stop, I press unto great things stored
At the corner of the rainbow leading to the pot of gold.

I march into the greatness I was created for
I latch unto the highway of my success
The valleys and mountains, failures and gorges stop me not.
I breathe the fresh air of creativity

It digests every doubt or fear stored within
My nucleus explodes into a Pandora of purpose.

I spring forth and march into the greatness of my time
The flowers bloom and the scents are beautiful
The butterflies sense what is slowly becoming
The lilies of the valley slowly populate the landscape
The bare branches bring forth the seeds for the new season.

My latter shall be greater than my former.
I am a child of destiny, a child of purpose.
I have a divine nature and I exhibit my kind
I march into the greatness of time
I march into the greatness of my time.

## The Orchids of Catalina

The rooftops glitter in the mid-day sun.
Densely populated and loosely regulated.
Confused and hungry wondering where helps lies.
The dogs stroll aimlessly in the street.

The traffic goes in every direction grinding to an abrupt stop.
There is a motionless body on the street,
Citizens walk by oblivious of the lifeless presence.
A far too common site and a fixture to a restive lifestyle.

Accepted as the way of life for a people caught in the crossfire.
The police finally show up.
Caution tapes keeps onlookers at bay.
They ask a few questions and leave without an arrest.

They dump John Doe on the bed of the truck
An end to another promising soul.
I hold in my hand the orchid of Catalina.
The beauty captivates and the fragrance invites.

The lush vegetation is a great backdrop for life.
Something so beautiful lies within the carnage.
The movements of the populace are delayed.
Thinking twice before every step.

There are constant reminders of a country devoid of peace.
We used to be a simple-minded bunch.
Now we are a few steps away from the grave.
There are holes in every wall.

A lasting monument to the gangs that rule.
The birds have stopped perching on the rooftops.
They peer from a safe distance.
The kids are now men.

They age too soon and lose their innocence.
Playgrounds are empty and overgrown with brush.
Dreams and nightmares are a constant companion.
Forced silence is the order of the day.

Any slip and you might slip into the unknown.
We have seen so much, but say very little.
Sometimes, we just wait for the fumes from the kettle.
Every now and then, I escape into an imaginary world.

I dare into the field and pluck a rich and vibrant orchid.
The smell reminds me of the path to the future,
A place of peace and nostalgia hidden within.
Inviting you into fields of Gold.

The stem is long and variegated.
The buds are like the template of an artist.
It blossoms every season, in war and peace.
A constant reminder of an environment in flux.

It dots the landscape close to the riverbed.
The frogs hide and seek within the valley.
I tug and roll into forgetfulness.
An ideal escape valve for my soul.

I hold it high and it glitters in the Sun.
The colors are so soft and innocent.
A present and hope for my spirit.
The beautiful orchid of Catalina.

# The Presence of Absence (9-11)

It was a clear beautiful day.
The sky was blue and all seemed cool.
The clouds were tucked neatly within the frame of normalcy.
The birds sang happily as they raced from the roofs and treetops.

Several people woke up and said goodbye to their kids and loved ones
They carried suitcases and briefcases
Planning for the day that lay ahead.
Some left without saying a thing,

The morn was still asleep when the door was shut.
They began the journey of no return
Lacking the knowledge of predestination?
Twisted Fate in Juxtaposition.

The plot had been in the works for some years.
Young men who decided their cause were worth killing for.
They plotted the strategy of destruction in hotel rooms and schools.
They practiced the art of flying
For the sake of spilling the blood of the innocent.

The plotter and the plotted were headed for a fatal twist of fate.
They boarded flights and left for their daily grind.
Some were young and dependent while others had paid their dues
They all headed for the intersection of the great beyond.

The planes took to the sky on a normal day.
The pilots made the announcements with the usual greeting.
And then, suddenly several men stood up and held everybody hostage.
They threatened and stabbed some in the process of subduing most.

The flight plan was changed for a path of the collision of destiny.
The date was Nine Eleven forever enshrined in our collective minds.
The hijackers commandeered the birds

And flew right into the world trade center.
Thousands of lives were lost in the carnage and destruction.

The twin towers were once the center of hustle and Bustle.
A testament to the ingenuity of Man.
Many called it home away from home.
In the twinkling of a moment, it tilted to the side,
Time stood still; and then it all came crashing down.

Lives that were born out of the will
Of most were destroyed by the hate of some.
The fire was so hot, that some jumped
From the window into the hands of angels.

First responders that went in to save
Could not be saved when the towers fell.
They made the ultimate sacrifice on
The account for service to humanity.

Today we remember the lost and especially the living.
We are determined to forge ahead in the midst of the loss.
We plant the seeds of a new generation and hoist a new flag.
Despite the security changes, we refuse to change our collective purpose.

Freedom and Justice for all is at the core of our being.
We observe a few seconds of silence to the sacrifice of the Lambs.
At the grounds of Ground zero,
There is a legacy of the presence of absence.

## The Telephone

Borne out of a single thought.
Talking to another at the end of the line.
Voices traveling the distance bearing a message.
Giving birth to a revolution that still remains.

It's the bearer of good tidings.
The town crier for sorrow.
The arbiter of good fortunes
The spark of young romances.

There was a time it was analog.
Dials and ring tones
Numbers and area codes
Telephone poles and telegraph.

Those were the days.
Who needs a telephone to make a call?
A phone dialer or viber will do the trick.
Long distances is now near distances
The world is now a global village.
Technology called Voice over I.P.

Talking is almost out and texting is in.
Why talk, when I can type.
Face booking, tweeting and tumble ring
It helps to foster human understanding.

A bold new world.
Apple, Androids, Blackberry or Microsoft
Were borne out of the advent of the telephone.
Changing constantly yet evoking upgrades.
To remain relevant, we keep spending!

## To Tie The Knot?

To tie the Knot?
You must be nuts.
To be stuck for the rest of your life
living in suspense every single second
tied at the hip to a person so petty?

I look around and I mostly see pain
Broken vehicles in need of repair
Relationships in comatose full of vinegar.
They said it would work, live happily ever after
just to see them falter a mile down the happy lane.

We try to talk, but the words are scarce and few.
I sometimes wonder how we said "I DO"
We stare and wear the look of disdain
to a person I once called my lion in the den.

The touch has given way to a slouch
on his favorite lifeless couch
He clings to the remote more than he clings to me
all he eats is popcorn and soda pops.

It used to be fairytales
A prince coming for his beautiful princess
The Rose has faded and the petals are falling
There was a time not long ago, all he fell for was me.

I looked in his eyes and all it shows is a blank stare
at the wall, table, window and all but my flare
I spoke but hit a hard wall
So hard, it bruises deep into my very soul.

The kids want him back
they want the Dad and not the Father
The one who played at the back with smiles and goof ball
He used to roll on the floor with the Family pet.

All they can get is just a tiny snippet
of a man who once was.
I tried not to, but I still love him
No matter what I do or think.

The feelings still resonate in my soul
there was once a time when he promised now and after.
In spite of it all, I still love you.

# Valet Driver

I am a Valet Driver.
I provide the best Hospitality
Experience for my guest.
I open the doors; welcome them
With a firm handshake and a smile.

Having a great attitude
During the interaction is what I practice.
My goal is to be the best Valet in the world.
I know the way to Please.

My Motto is 'run fast and drive slow'.
When I get a 'Pull', which is a request for a vehicle,
I dash toward the location with a sense of urgency.
While delivering the vehicle I maintain speed limit.
Looking out for people and Vehicles.

I am a student at Training Workforce University.
Majoring in Valet Sciences,
With a minor in high-powered interaction.
And the 15-5 Rule.

Required courses include,
Assistance technology,
Appreciation mathematics
And Appearance ergonomics.

While parking a car in space,
I check for existing damages.
I conduct a quick inspection
Of the vehicle and mark the ticket.

Any damage is brought
To the attention of the guest.
Valet experience
Is the best experience in Hospitality.

As a valet, I know how to drive a stick shift.
Most expensive sports cars
Come standard with manual transmission.
Guests are always impressed
When you treat their cars with extreme care.

They say thank you by offering a 'Tip'.
There is no magic formula
For the amount that is appropriate
It ranges from Zero to infinity.
If you are at your best,
You could be pleasantly surprised.

We work as a team.
When we are waiting to serve, we Post up.
Posting enables us to be attentive to guest needs.
It telegraphs to the guests
That we are attentive to their needs.

I pledge to be clean-shaven
And properly groomed.
Our appearance speaks volumes
About our willingness to exceed.

Clean and crisp,
We should always look and act the part.
I am a Valet Driver
And I am the best at what I do.

## What a Year!

A year filled with exhilaration.
A year filled with utter desolation.
We heard the cries of babes
And the final sigh of desperate souls.

It was the year of movements.
The occupy movement.
Moving and shaking everything in Society
Holding captive our collective conscience.

Going in every direction,
Appealing to the high and Low,
Changing the lingua Franca through the occupation.

We were introduced to 'easing',
Quantitative easing to be exact.
Easing away the pain with more
Of everything you can imagine
At the every end, the pain still remains.

Hurricanes were ever-present.
'Irene' left a mark on so many.
Earthquakes leveled years of labor,
Flattened all, as far as the eyes could see.
Floods bellowed and swallowed
Entire towns and villages.
Streets are now rivers for canoes and tugboats.

It was a year of 'NO'
No matter what passed through Congress,
It was always a predictable 'No'.
How could it be 'No', When so many

Yearned for a simple 'Yes' to survive?
The embers of recession fanned
Through the United States,
Across the Atlantic to Europe.

Bringing pain to the 'PIGS'
Hurting the very people who still
Wonder who gave a bad check,
Selling them into a band of slavery.

So many Homeless, So many.
So many Hungry, So many.
So many Jobless, So many.
So many Hopeless, So many.

A year that oversaw the falling of dictators
They once held sway over a defenseless populace,
Lashing out decrees with reckless abandon.
Jailing and maiming any that dared speak.

They soon discovered, it was a house of cards,
Crumbling at the behest of the rising of the oppressed.
From Egypt to Tunisia and on to Syria,
There is no stopping the train of Freedom.

'Fukishima' was a reminder to take heed,
We are the guardians of knowledge of life and death.
It hangs in the balance and we tip the scale.
We have the capacity to do good, we should.
It lifts our spirit higher than our dreams.
The earth is fragile and we are the custodians.

Despite it all, we trudge along.
Carrying the weights and burdens,
Sacrificing our very existence,
Speaking in silence,

Crying through the Laughter,
Giving through the Lack.
Through it all, we remain.
By his grace, we maintain.

By his Love, we are sustained.
By Faith, we welcome the New Year.
Away with the Old and longing for the New.
Happy New Year to you Indeed!

## Where Do I Start?

I lay there thinking about it all.
Wondering what I should do next?
I try to hide in the hole dug last night.
Wishing someone, somewhere, somehow will help.

Help never came and I sank further.
Sliding down the slippery slopes.
Mudslides customized for my situation.
Muddied and bloodied during the fall.

At the bottom, I wonder if I should get up.
Is it worth it to make another move?
It's safer and better to stay still.
Not moving but sighing through the pain.

I realize that all this while,
The courage and declarations of confidence
Slides through the inner demons
Building on the confidence of yesterday.
I will start from the beginning.
With a single step.

# Who is This Boy?

Before he was born he was known
After his birth he was made known
To know him is to love him
To love him is to know him
In him was life a way of life as a guide.

The light shines so bright
There is no darkness in or around him.
They brought him gifts but he was the gift
The gift of life to have and to hold
He gives it to all that asks.

He heals the sick, he calms the sea
He sees through the very dark days
The days are his
He is the first and the last in one.

He forms and he reforms
His form is the three in one
He is the one that was awaited
He is the one that we still awaits
The Son of the most high.

Why not fight and declare your lordship?
Born into royalty
But borne the weight of our courtship
He knows my innermost emotions
Mostly tempered by his ever-loving kindness.

He rules but chose to ride on a mule
Gentle and mellow,
I trust him so much,
What a great bedfellow.

You know, I thought I had arrived
At the place of comfort so bright
A wonderful locale by the streams
Lush gardens and beautiful greenery.

I am constantly reminded that the imagery
Should not be what is before me, but ahead of me
A place I hardly know, a place born in my dreams.
I bow and wait at the soon coming king.

He wears no earthly crown
I sing and Praise
of his goodness and mercies
On a daily basis.

So much, I can hardly count
It mounts every second
In May, the flowers bloom
Transformative mixture
Of sweat and blood.